A Father's Book of Wisdom

Compiled by H. Jackson Brown, Jr.

Rutledge Hill Press
Nashville, Tennessee

Published in Nashville, Tennessee by Rutledge Hill Press, Inc., 211 Seventh Avenue North, Nashville, Tennessee 37219. Distributed in Canada by H.B. Fenn and Company, Ltd., 1090 Lorimar Dr., Mississauga, Ontario L5S IR7. Distributed in Australia by Millennium Books, 13/3 Maddox Street, Alexandria NSW 2015. Distributed in New Zealand by Tandem Press, 2 Rugby Road, Birkenhead, Auckland 10. Distributed in the United Kingdom by Verulam Publishing, Ltd., 152a Park Street Lane, Park Street, St. Albans, Hertfordshire AL2 2AU.

Typography by D & T / Bailey, Nashville, Tennessee

Library of Congress Cataloging-in-Publication Data

A Father's book of wisdom / compiled by Jack Brown
p. cm.
ISBN 1-55853-107-6
I. Quotations, English. I. Brown, Jack, 1940-
PN6081.F33 1989
082 — dc19 89-3517
CIP

Printed in the United States of America
13 14 15 16 — 99 98 97 96

A Parable

A FEW WEEKS after Dad passed away, we found eight shoeboxes in his closet. They were filled with scraps of paper, old envelopes, napkins, matchbook covers, little blue spiral notebooks—even cash register receipts—all covered with ideas Dad thought were profound, interesting, or merely amusing. Obviously, Dad had grabbed whatever paper was available whenever he had felt inspired.

Some of the notes were quotations from books and articles he had read, but many were original insights and observations.

Dad had always been a reader, a thinker, a kitchen-table philosopher. We were thrilled to discover this rich legacy of his intellect, wit, and wisdom.

We sorted through all the writings and compiled this book. It's a book about one father's view of life and what he thought about the importance of self-reliance, commitment, love, generosity, and success.

We hope you'll enjoy reading it. Dad never told us how to be successful and happy—he just gave us the opportunity to watch him do it.

Contents

Other books by H. Jackson Brown, Jr.

P.S. I Love You
Life's Little Instruction Book
Live and Learn and Pass It On
Life's Little Instruction Book, Volume II
Life's Little Treasure Book On Joy
Life's Little Treasure Book On Marriage and Family
Life's Little Treasure Book On Wisdom
Life's Little Treasure Book On Success
Life's Little Treasure Book On Parenting
Life's Little Treasure Book On Love
When You Lick A Slug, Your Tongue Goes Numb
The Little Book of Christmas Joys
(with Rosemary Brown and Kathy Peel)
Live and Learn and Pass It On, Volume II
Life's Little Instruction Book, Volume III

DON'T let
what you cannot do
interfere with what
you can do.

—John Wooden

Pride makes
us do things well.
But it is love that makes us
do them to perfection.

—Dad

WINNING is not a
sometime thing;
it's an all-time thing.
You don't win once in a while,
you don't do things right once
in a while, you do them right
all the time. Winning is a habit.
Unfortunately, so is losing.

—*Vince Lombardi*

THE harder you work,
the luckier you get.

—Gary Player

BEHOLD the turtle.
He makes progress only
when he sticks his neck out.

—James B. Conant

THE secret is
to become wise
before you get old.

—Dad

FIRST you forget names,
then you forget faces,
then you forget to pull
your zipper up, then you forget to
pull your zipper down.

—Leo Rosenburg

WHEN you were born,
you cried and the world rejoiced.
Live your life in such a manner that
when you die the world cries
and you rejoice.

—Old Indian Saying

WHEN an
old person dies,
a library is lost.

—Tommy Swann

THERE is nothing
either good or bad,
but thinking makes it so.

—*William Shakespeare*

To travel
hopefully is better
than to arrive.

—Sir James Jeans

TWO stonecutters were
asked what they were doing.
The first said, "I'm cutting
this stone into blocks."
The second replied, "I'm on a
team that's building a cathedral."

—*Old Story*

REGARDLESS of what
company you work for,
never forget the most important
product you're selling
is yourself.

—*Dad*

WHEN you
dance with your customer,
let him lead.

—Dad

CHALLENGES can
be stepping stones
or stumbling blocks.
It's just a matter of
how you view them.

—Unknown

I AM only one;
but still I am one.
I cannot do everything,
but still I can do something;
I will not refuse to do
the something I can do.

—Helen Keller

IN matters of style,
swim with the current;
in matters of principle,
stand like a rock.

—*Thomas Jefferson*

WHEN the
One Great Scorer comes
to write against your name,
He marks, not that you won
or lost, but how you
played the game.

—Grantland Rice

If you don't
stand for something,
you'll fall for anything.

—*Unknown*

HOLD yourself
responsible for a higher standard
than anyone else expects of you.
Never excuse yourself.

—Henry Ward Beecher

IF you were
to sell your character,
would you get full retail,
or would it go for a bargain-
basement price?

—Dad

YOU never
know a man's character
until you've shared a bowl of
peeled shrimp with him.

—*Dad*

COURAGE is
resistance to fear,
mastery of fear,
not absence of fear.

—Mark Twain

DON'T be
afraid to take big steps.
You can't cross a chasm
in two small jumps.

—*David Lloyd George*

WHAT matters
is not the size of the dog
in the fight, but the size
of the fight in the dog.

—Coach Bear Bryant

ONE man
with courage makes
a majority.

—Andrew Jackson

IF you
judge people,
you have no time
to love them.

—Mother Teresa

WHEN you
judge others, you are
revealing your own fears
and prejudices.

—Dad

I WILL
speak ill of no man,
and speak all the good I
know of everybody.

—*Benjamin Franklin*

LET the
refining and improving
of your own life keep you so busy
that you have little time
to criticize others.

—*Dad*

PRAISE
in public.
Criticize in
private.

—Dad

WE'RE constantly striving for success, fame, and comfort when all we really need to be happy is someone or something to be enthusiastic about.

—*Dad*

A GROUP OF
two hundred executives were asked
what makes a person successful.
Eighty percent listed enthusiasm as
the most important quality.

—Source Unknown

EXCELLENCE
is never an
accident.

—*Dad*

OH, the difference
between nearly right
and exactly right.

—Dad

THE quality
of a person's life is in
direct proportion to their
commitment to excellence,
regardless of their chosen
field of endeavor.

—*Vince Lombardi*

IT'S a funny
thing about life;
if you refuse to accept
anything but the best,
you very often
get it.

—Somerset Maugham

WELL done
is better than
well said.

—*Benjamin Franklin*

IT'S not
how far you fall,
but how high you
bounce.

—Dad

SOME goals
are so worthy,
it's glorious even
to fail.

—Unknown

IF your life
is free of failures,
you're not taking
enough risks.

—Dad

DON'T judge
those who try and fail.
Judge only those who
fail to try.

—Dad

WHEN you
have been wronged,
a poor memory is your
best response.

—Dad

DON'T carry a grudge.
While you're carrying the grudge
the other guy's out dancing.

—*Buddy Hackett*

FORGIVE and forget.
Sour grapes make for
a lousy wine.

—Dad

Do not
use a hatchet to remove
a fly from your friend's
forehead.

—Chinese Proverb

A FRIEND
is a gift you give
yourself.

—Robert Louis Stevenson

To have
a friend, be
a friend.

—Old Saying

HAPPINESS is
not an absence of problems,
but the ability to deal
with them.

—Dad

MOST people
are about as happy as
they make up their minds
to be.

—*Abraham Lincoln*

SUCCESS is
getting what you want.
Happiness is liking
what you get.

—Dad

TO be without
some of the things you want
is an indispensable part
of happiness.

—Bertrand Russell

HAPPINESS
is an inside job.

—Dad

PREFER a loss
to a dishonest gain;
the one brings pain at
the moment, the other
for all time.

—*Chilton*

DISHONESTY
is like a boomerang.
About the time you think all
is well, it hits you in the
back of the head.

—*Dad*

No legacy
is so rich as
honesty.

—*William Shakespeare*

WHEN you
tell the truth, you never
have to worry about your
lousy memory.

—Dad

HONESTY
is the first chapter
in the book of
wisdom.

—Thomas Jefferson

MAN'S mind,
once stretched by a new idea,
never regains its original
dimension.

—Oliver Wendell Holmes

YOU see things
that are and say, "Why?"
But I dream things that never were
and say, "Why not?"

—*George Bernard Shaw*

IMAGINATION
is more important
than knowledge.

—Albert Einstein

ALWAYS
be a little kinder
than necessary.

—James M. Barrie

THERE are
no unimportant jobs,
no unimportant people,
no unimportant acts
of kindness.

—*Dad*

THERE is
no experience better for
the heart than reaching down
and lifting people up.

—John Andrew Holmer

I EXPECT
to pass through life but once.
If, therefore, there be any kindness
I can show, or any good thing
I can do to any fellow being, let me
do it now, for I shall not
pass this way again.

—*William Penn*

THIS is the
final test of a gentleman:
his respect for those who can
be of no possible value
to him.

—*William Lyon Phelps*

THE smallest
act of kindness is worth
more than the grandest
intention.

—*Dad*

REAL generosity
is doing something nice
for someone who'll never
find it out.

—Frank A. Clark

NEVER let
a day go by without
giving at least three people
a compliment.

—*Dad*

WE don't
know one millionth
of one percent about
anything.

—*Thomas Edison*

ALL that
mankind has ever learned is
nothing more than a single grain
of sand on a beach that reaches
to infinity.

—Dad

THE manager administers, the leader innovates. The manager maintains, the leader develops. The manager relies on systems, the leader relies on people. The manager counts on controls, the leader counts on trust. The manager does things right, the leader does the right thing.

—*Fortune Magazine*

LOVE doesn't
sit there like a stone,
it has to be made, like bread;
remade all the time,
made new.

—Ursula K. Le Guin

TREASURE the
love you receive above all.
It will survive long after your
gold and good health
have vanished.

—Og Mandino

WHO,
being loved,
is poor?

—Oscar Wilde

YOU will find
as you look back upon your life
that the moments when you have
really lived are the moments
when you have done things
in the spirit of love.

—Henry Drummond

Men always
want to be a woman's first love;
women have a more subtle instinct:
what they like is to be a man's
last romance.

—*Unknown*

FOR an instant,
love can transform
the world.

—*Dad*

WE two
form a multitude.

—*Ovid*

MARRIAGE
is an empty box.
It remains empty unless
you put in more than
you take out.

—Dad

BY all means marry;
if you get a good wife, you'll
become happy; if you get a
bad one, you'll become
a philosopher.

—*Socrates*

If you're
looking for a big opportunity,
seek out a big
problem.

—*Dad*

A WISE man
will make more opportunities
than he finds.

—Francis Bacon

PROBLEMS
are opportunities
in work clothes.

—Henry Kaiser

In the
middle of difficulty
lies opportunity.

—Albert Einstein

THERE is
no future in any job.
The future lies in the
man who holds
the job.

—*George Crane*

Don't wait
for your ship to come in.
Row out to meet it.

—Dad

THERE is
only one pretty child
in the world, and every
mother has it.

—Chinese Proverb

FATHERS are
pals nowadays because
they don't have the guts
to be fathers.

—*Dad*

WHEN I was
a boy of fourteen, my father was
so ignorant I could hardly stand
to have the old man around.
But when I got to be twenty-one,
I was astonished at how
much he had learned
in seven years.

—Mark Twain

TRAIN up
a child in the way he should go,
and when he is old, he
will not depart
from it.

—*Proverbs 22:6*

A FATHER
is a banker provided
by nature.

—*French Proverb*

In the
game of life even
the 50-yard line seats
don't interest me.
I came to play!

—Dad

Do it!
Move it! Make it happen!
No one ever sat their way
to success.

—Dad

NOTHING in the world
can take the place of persistence.
Talent will not; nothing is more
common than unsuccessful men
with talent. Genius will not;
unrewarded genius is almost
a proverb. Education will not;
the world is full of educated failures.
Persistence and determination alone
are omnipotent.

—*Calvin Coolidge*

SUCCESS
seems to be largely
a matter of hanging on
after others have
let go.

—William Feather

IN the confrontation
between the stream and the rock,
the stream always wins—not through
strength but by
perseverance.

—*Dad*

THE man
who wins may have
been counted out several times,
but he didn't hear
the referee.

—*H. E. Jansen*

NEVER,
never, never, never
give up.

—Winston Churchill

WE do not
see things as they are.
We see things
as we are.

—Dad

OUR thoughts
determine our responses to life.
We are not victims of the world.
To the extent that we
control our thoughts,
we control the world.

—*Dad*

WHAT you
see is what you get—
except in pre-packaged
strawberries.

—*Dad*

THE display
of status symbols is
usually a result of low self-esteem.
The self-confident person can afford
to project a modest image.

—*Dad*

NO one
can make you feel
inferior without your
consent.

—Eleanor Roosevelt

ALWAYS consider yourself
a first-class citizen of the world.
No one deserves better treatment than
you.

—Dad

BE good
to yourself. Be patient.
Be kind. Be forgiving.
After all, you're all
you've got.

—Dad

THE closest
we ever come to perfection
is when we write
our résumés.

—Dad

SEND someone a
telegram that reads
"Congratulations."
Regardless of who he is,
he'll think he's done something
the past week to deserve it.

—*Dad*

WHEN an archer
misses the mark, he turns and
looks for the fault within himself.
Failure to hit the bull's-eye is
never the fault of the target.
To improve your aim—
improve yourself.

—*Gilbert Arland*

SELF-RELIANCE
is the greatest gift
a parent can give
a child.

—*Dad*

SELF-RELIANCE
is like a flashlight;
no matter how dark it gets,
it will help you find
your way.

—Dad

YOU are
free the moment you
do not look outside yourself
for someone to solve
your problems.

—Dad

Not in time,
place, or circumstance,
but in the man
lies success.

—Charles Rouce

HE has
achieved success
who has lived well,
laughed often, and
loved much.

—*Bessie Anderson Stanley.*

ANY failure
will tell you
success is nothing
but luck.

—*Dad*

FAILURE is success
if we learn from it.

—Malcolm S. Forbes

SUCCESS is
best measured by
how far you've come
with the talents you've
been given.

—*Dad*

THE road
to success is not
doing one thing 100 percent better,
but doing 100 things one
percent better.

—*Dad*

BEHIND every
successful man
stands a proud wife
and surprised
mother-in-law.

—Brooks Hays

Success
comes before work
only in the
dictionary.

—Anonymous

WE make
a living by what we get,
but we make a life by
what we give.

—*Norman MacEwan*

THE true
measure of success
is not what you have,
but what you can
do without.

—*Dad*

THERE is
never a wrong
time to do the
right thing.

—Dad

I'D rather
have roses on my table
than diamonds on
my neck.

—Emma Goldman

IT'S not
hard to make decisions
when you know what
your values are.

—*Roy Disney*

I'D like
to be rich enough so
I could throw soap away
after the letters are
worn off.

—*Andy Rooney*

I'M opposed
to millionaires, but
it would be dangerous
to offer me the
position.

—Mark Twain

WEALTHY people
miss one of life's great
thrills—making the last
car payment.

—Dad

If you
pick up a starving dog
and make him prosperous,
he will not bite you.
This is the principal
difference between a
dog and a man.

—*Mark Twain*

Choose a
job you love, and
you will never have
to work a day
in your life.

—*Confucius*

More people
rust out than
wear out.

—Dad

THE biggest
mistake you can make
is to believe that you work
for someone else.

—Unknown

GOD
gives the nuts,
but He does not
crack them.

—Old Proverb

IF you work
for a man, in Heaven's name
work for him! If he pays you
wages that supply your bread
and butter, work for him,
stand by him, and stand by
the institution he represents.

—*Elbert Hubbard*

WORK
well done
is art.

—Dad

WHEN you
can't change the
direction of the wind—
adjust your sails.

—*Dad*

YOU are
the same today that
you'll be five years from now
except for two things:
the people you meet
and the books
you read.

—Mac McMillan

PEOPLE who
are resting on their laurels
are wearing them on
the wrong end.

—*Unknown*

HOW to Make a Speech:
Be Sincere
Be Brief
Be Seated

—Dad

ART is
man's attempt
to improve on
nature.

—Dad

THERE are
two times in a man's
life when he should not speculate:
when he can't afford it,
and when he can."

—Mark Twain

NO one
ever went broke
saving money.

—Dad

To his dog,
every man is Napoleon;
hence, the constant popularity
of dogs.

—Unknown

EACH man
has a choice in life:
he may approach it
as a creator or critic,
a lover or a hater,
a giver or a taker.

—*Unknown*

THE greatest
ignorance is to reject
something you know
nothing about.

—*Dad*

LET your
policy be
quality.

—Dad

A DIAMOND
is a chunk of coal
that made good
under pressure.

—*Anonymous*

LAUGHTER
has no foreign
accent.

—Paul Lowney

THE man
with imagination is
never alone.

—Dad

To teach
is to learn
again.

—Dad

EVEN if
you're on the right track,
you'll get run over
if you just
sit there.

—*Will Rogers*

YOU never
get a second chance
to make a good first
impression.

—*Dad*

LIFE doesn't come
with an instruction book—
that's why we
have fathers.

—*Dad*